Fleabite Scabs - anti-poetry #1

Screams from the Gig Economy

Published by Red Raw
London UK
www.red-raw.org
ISBN: 9780955704468
All rights reserved © 2022

P.4 -   Fleabite Scabs
P.6 -   Looking for Love in All the Wrong Places
P.8 -   Just Another Damned Couple
P.10 - Fucking Petals
P.12 - If You Drop Dead
P.14 - That Pink Woollen Suit
P.16 - Honeymoon Hell
P.18 - Cheap Wine & Crushed Dreams
P.20 - The Things We Do for Love
P.22 - The Price You Pay
P.24 - Like Two Dogs in the Park
P.27 - With the Strays and the Thieves
P.29 - That Idiot Was Me
P.31 - I Parked the Car in a Hedge
P.33 - A Couple of Losers
P.35 - Overweight and Over Forty
P.37 - The Hangover
P.39 - Petrol Days and Petrol Nights
P.41 - Drunk by the Bridge

P.43 - Dancing at the Trades Hall Social Club

P.45 - The Most Beautiful Place in Bruges

P.47 - Dual Fuel Tariff

P.59 - Slam the Door

P.52 - One For the Kids

P.54 - Half Past Ten on a Sunday Night

P.56 - The Beauty of Litter

Fleabite Scabs

They looked like fleabite scabs on her
ankles
She had a chipped-tooth smile
A bent back
And smelt of tomorrow's laundry basket
Today

But when she said
The clothes dumped outside Oxfam
Looked like a bed of flowers
I noticed that her lips were prettier
Than anyone else's in the pub that night
And her flea-bitten ankles had shape
So I offered to buy her a drink

Anyone who thought rags
Strewn along the path
Looked like roses in bloom
Was worth half a Stella any day of the week

Looking for Love in All the Wrong Places

I saw you drop my steak on the floor
Saw it land on the filthy tiles
Then you picked it up
Blew on it and
Slammed it back on the plate
Before calling me in to eat
Man, that steak tasted good

And over dinner
With the potatoes half burnt
Half mush
You told me
You'd been through my knicker-drawer
And thrown out all the raggy pants
All the ones with holes in them
Like it was an act of love
Like it was the most romantic thing ever

And on the sofa
Watching DIY on Channel 5
You said
D'ye remember that shelf you GLUED to the wall?
I told you not to put anything on it, I said
Nothing but herbs
Jesus Christ, the noise it made
Crashing to the floor
All those pots and pans
Smashing and clanging

And last thing at night
While we're putting out the trash
We could hear a police helicopter hovering above
Its searchlight scanning the barren bedrooms below
Looking for love, you said
Looking for things you find written in a valentine's card
If they are, I said
They're looking in all the wrong places

Just Another Damned Couple

When we landed in Rome
I was wearing a hangover
Like a brain haemorrhage
And you had a boil on your cheek
That had the hotel desk staring at us
Checking our passports
Checking the dates
Before handing over the key and
Pointing to the lift

As far as they were concerned
We were just another damned couple
In a cheap hotel
But up in the room we didn't feel so bad

In fact, we felt blessed and
With the horns blaring outside
We got into bed and made everything
feel right

After we were done
I leaned over and
Cleaned my dirty glasses
With your dirty pants and
Took a good look at your
Shattered face
The boil was raging
Hard and red
There was a stink of stomach
Coming off of you
But you never looked more lovely
And the world never felt better
Than it did right then
No, never better

Fucking Petals

Still drunk, I fall into the bathroom
Send a flowerpot crashing to the floor
What's HAPPENING, you shout from the bed
What ye DOING in there?
NOTHING, I shout back
Shoving the pot back on the shelf

The floor is spotted with bright red petals
Like Hammer House blood on the godless tiles
But I know you won't like it
So I scoop them up
Dump them in the pan

In with the used paper and the crap
In with the fumes of stinking hell
Then I pull the chain and
Flush it all away

Back in the room
Where a cloud of broken promises
Hangs low over the bed
I crawl back under the covers
And close my eyes

Ten minutes later you're up
And I can hear you cursing
Cursing the day you ever laid eyes on
me ... *THE STATE OF THE PLACE*
Then you're back at the door
Demanding to know
What all that MESS is
All that DIRT on the floor
All those FUCKING PETALS in the pan
They're for you, I manage to say
I put them there for you
For a princess

If You Drop Dead

If you drop dead
I'll bury you in those horrible boots
And that jacket your Mum got you
Yes, THAT one
The one you never wear

If you drop dead
I'll lean over the coffin
Like I'm going for a last kiss
And whisper *fuck you*
Right into your face

If you drop dead
I'll delete your number on my phone

YES I WILL
And give all your clothes to Betty
And get rid of the cat

If you drop dead
I don't know what I'd do

That Pink Woollen Suit

You left me
Three weeks before Christmas
Left me lying on the bed thinking about
Love gone wrong
Going to Paris, you cried
Wearing that pink woollen suit
A few things rammed in a case
Getting out of here, you cried
Because you're a *FU-CKING-AR-SOLE*

It was your birthday
I'd drunk too much
Drunk too fast
We both had

But it was me who fell over
Me who landed on the table
And got us thrown out of the place

Lying on the bed thinking about
Love gone wrong
I hoped you'd be safe out there
With all the drunks out there
But most of all I hoped you'd come back
And forgive me
For all those unforgivable things

And an hour later
THANK GOD
The door burst open and
The light flashed on
You came crashing into the room
Like a bull
A steaming bull
Warning me not to say a word
NOT ONE FUCKING WORD
And got into bed
Wearing that pink woollen suit

Honeymoon Hell

Ah Napoli, we'll never forget
The smell of garlic and sewers
And that kid on a scooter
Dragging you down the street
Pulling at your bag
With me screaming *YOU TWAT*
At his empty-handed back

The next day we got the coach out of there
Drove past the grapes and the groves
Past the villages and dogs
And African prostitutes
Selling rape in the bushes

For 30 Euros a shot
OH MY GOD, you moaned
OH MY GOD
But then said nothing
NOTHING
All the way to the coast

Ah Sorrento, we'll never forget
The honey hotels on sea-cliff streets
And that spikey black thing
That clinging to the rock thing
That stabbed you in the hand
Made your fingers swell like ginger

The chemist marched us to a jeweller
Who cut off your rings
And made the sign of the cross
Like there was a curse on our marriage
Like it was already FUCKING DOOMED
Jesus Christ, you yelled
What next?
Nothing, I said, like I knew of a plan
Nothing
But when you turned away
I made the sign of the cross too

Cheap Wine and Crushed Dreams

Dancing drunk to Bacharach at two in
the morning
Dancing drunk with a stain on my pants
Your bra strap hanging down
And when Cilla sings
What's It All About, Alfie?
We look at each other and shake our
heads

Our boy, crashed out on the floor
Our girl, God knows where
The cat, scraping at the take-away tray
And then there's me

And there's you
Still clinging to something
Decades down the line

Yeah, we've had our days of taxicabs
and butter
We've had our chances
But right now
Right now ...
Aaahhhh ...
WHAT THE HELL

When you're this far gone
On cheap wine and crushed dreams
You take whatever you can get

The Things We Do for Love

Cabaret
The Savoy Theatre
I don't know what I'm doing here
But here I am
Slouching on the front row
Like a defrocked priest
Searching for a new God

You're next to me
Dressed in herringbone and
Loving every minute of this
This ... FUCKING SHOW

And I act too

Act like I really enjoy it
Even if I'm strapped to a table
Being butchered alive

The star is inches away from us
Horrid make-up caked all over his skull

Prancing around in leather shorts
LEATHER for Christ's sake
Singing
Money Makes the World Go Around
And stuffing dollar bills into his mouth

And then
When he spits them out
One flies my way and
Hits me on the chest
And I wonder if he aimed it at me
If he wants to escape this torment too

Christ Almighty, I mutter
The things we do for love

The Price You Pay

You wanted Chanel No 5
But I didn't have the money
Didn't want to spend the money
So I got you a bottle of Baileys instead

And when you opened it
You said you loved it
You even dabbed some
Behind your ears
And I licked it off

But now
Every time that ad comes on the TV
Every time that model

Walks through the golden light
I can't look at you
Because I know what you're thinking

I swear to God
If I could go back
I'd sell the car
I'd sell a **FUCKING KIDNEY**
Just to see you open the box

Two Dogs in the Park

Heavy with beer and curry
Fumbling with her jacket
With her keys
She opened the door and told me to open the wine
While she placed coloured scarves over the lamps
The music was moany and
She danced around the room
Like a bin bag caught in a tree
Her whipping hair and swirling hands
Created terrifying shadows across the walls
And it was something to watch

I'll give her that
Something even a gypsy would've
clapped along to
But at the same time
It began to get on my nerves
So after another wailing scream
I grabbed hold of her waist
And mashed my dhansak lips
Right down into her face

Next thing you know I fell on a chair
And landed on a cat
A one-eyed thing
A hissy-bagpipe thing
That flew across the floor
Complaining and wailing until
She ran after it
Calling after it, *Smithy ... Smithy*

Eventually
When things had calmed down
She took me to bed
And we went at it like two dogs in the park
Driven mad by the scent

She whispered things in my ear
Things about her rosebud
Her lady lips

And when I joined in
Calling her a *DIRTY LITTLE FUCK SLUT*
She told me to stop right there
She didn't like any of that
Disgusting stuff
It made her feel cheap
And slow down, will you?
Don't be so rough

An hour later
Drained dry on her tie-dye bed
I wondered if there was a night bus I
could catch
What excuse I could give
That's when I saw the cat at the door
Its one-eyed head staring in at me
Hating me
Willing me to die like all the rest

I reached over, flicked off the lamp
Turned my face to the wall

With the Strays and the Thieves

I thought about you today
Thought about you again
I was passing through Finsbury Park
And wondered what you were doing
right now
Sleeping probably
Thousands of miles away
Next to your American wife

And it made me think of that summer
When you slept next to me
Next to that hut on the beach

With the strays and the thieves

The wind was in from Africa
Just like Joni said it was
And you had dreadlocks
A guitar and a sandpaper tan

It was back in the '80s
But I can see your teenage face
Clearer now
Than when we said goodbye
At Finsbury Park
Two months ago

That Idiot Was Me

Some idiot bought her a drink and
That idiot was me
A dancing drunk at the karaoke pub
With 50 in my pocket and 20 in my sock

And later on
When the music stopped
She took me back to her benefits hotel
Where the hallway stank of debt
And the rooms
Hid men and women
With nothing more than a mattress

A few old clothes and
A box full of bad decisions

And yes
I was another bad decision
We both knew that
But there was room in the box for one more

I opened a beer
As she took off her pants
And that's when I saw the devil
Tattooed into her backside
Like some branding stamp
On pudding flesh

I knew then
That this was where heaven met hell
And I was at the front of the queue
Ready to pay for my sinning ways

I Parked the Car in a Hedge

Coming back from the job
Hot and tired
I nearly run into some prick in a van
Screaming at me to get out of his way

I remember you once said that
If you meet more than one dickhead in
the day
Then the dickhead is you
Well, sometimes
It feels like
I don't have enough middle fingers

For this world

Back at the flat
I sit in the car and play our track
Blasting it out with the windows down
While the neighbour glares at me
Like I'm making her life a living hell
Like I have no respect
Singing and banging my fists on the wheel

But I miss you right now
I really do

Do you remember that time
I parked the car in a hedge
And you laughed till you cried?

Do you remember that time
You sobbed for an hour
When you found that photo of your Dad?

I miss you right now
I really do

A Couple of Losers

Watching whatever on the TV
You tell me you don't want to go to Vegas
Let's get married in Camden instead
That place near the zoo, you say
Where you can hear the lions roar
And let's do it now or it'll be too late

I look at you and think
It's already too late for us
All those plans of Elvis
And stretch limos

Well, they were just the stupid dreams of
a couple of losers

Remember that great idea we had
The one that was going to make us a
million?
At least the business plan
Helped us light the BBQ that night

And the prototype we made
The one with all the cables and the knobs
What sad fun we had smashing it to
pieces
After the third bottle of red

We hung our heads after that one
Hung them in catholic shame
Knowing we were destined for jobs
In office blocks and shops

But at least we have each other, I think
Me and you
With the roar of the lions
At that place near the zoo

Overweight and Over Forty

I saw her today
Hot pants so tight her cheeks were
Flapping out
And all the other mothers
With their brats and their bitter lives
Stared at her with mouths open wide

I saw her today
Walking to school in all that make up
Overweight and over forty
Click-clacking across the playground
Dragging it past them

I saw her in the bank
Her skirt riding high up her leg
Her chest swinging low
Her fat gut hanging over the belt

The meet-and-greet guy
Kept looking round
Kept turning his head
To make sure he'd actually seen
What he'd seen

I saw her in the street
Wearing those bling-bling heels
And nails so long
OH MY GOD
The length of them
The colour of them
I could just imagine them
Tearing at my back
At my face

I saw her today
At the checkout in Asda
Her daft kid sucking on biscuits
A bottle of wine and a fake Gucci bag

I saw her today and I thought
WOW

The Hangover

You're a bitch, I tell her
Nurse Bitch
Lying in bed
Shaking with booze fever
I stare at her like she's somebody
Nobody I know
And all I want her to do
Is get me some water
Get me some pills

She studies me in the mirror
Turns round and stares at me in the bed

Says, *I didn't want it to be like this*
But I've got something to tell you
I guess I'm in trouble
Guess she's ready to rain down the pain
Early March, she says
Early March what? I croak
That's when our baby's due

I jump up and grab her
I hug her tightly
And feel the room spinning
Both of us knowing that
Our lives have changed forever
Then I run to the bathroom
Put my head in the pan
And throw it all up

Petrol Days and Petrol Nights

On the 4-0-6 and the traffic is jammed
Nothing moving more than an inch
Nothing but the planes in the sky
The kids on the bridge
The snails on the wall

Up ahead, the brake lights flare
But my phone is dead
20 minutes late
And there's not a damn thing I can do
'cept pray you'll understand

The carcas of a fox lies in the gutter
A billboard poster shreds in the wind
The fuel gauge on red
And there's not a damn thing I can do
'cept wish you happy birthday

Petrol days and petrol nights

Drunk by the Bridge

Drunk by the bridge
In Camden Town and
Searching for the truth

Drunk by the bridge
When a wino appears
A real drinker
Dressed in rags and
Ranting about the canals
The bankers
The Good Lord above

Ye can SWIM to Manchester, he screams
Cleanse ye rotten souls in the canal
Redemption in a SEWER
Drunk by the bridge
I get to my feet and
Start to unbutton my shirt
I'm ready, I tell him
Which way's north?

But then
I feel your hand on my belt
Pulling me back
Saving me from the water
Saving me from the truth
Saving me again

Dancing at the Trades Hall Social Club

A line of zombies
A line of battery flat robots
Doing the heel toe shuffle
To the Achey-Breaky Heart
At the Trades Hall Social Club

And there at the end of the line is you
With your blue black hair
Your golden boots and
Your shaky-shake skirt

Ah, how you rock and you roll

Your chest bouncing
Your hips swaying
The life in your body
Burning up the floor

And all the women stare at you
Hate you
Because you are everything
They are not

And all the men stare at you
Love you
Because they remember
What it used to be like
When life was wet with sex

And when you swing it round
Your thighs flash in the light and
I've got to tell you, babe
I can't take my eyes off you either

The Most Beautiful Place in Bruges

A romantic break they called it
The canals
The churches
The beer
So we bought the tickets and
Packed our bags

When we got to the hotel
It was nothing more than an attic room
With a huge TV
And breakfast till 9

After a rest

We went out and did the canals
The cobbles
And God forgive us
We even took a horse and carriage
Round the streets
The city was beautiful
So beautiful that after an hour
I stopped seeing it and
It turned into one big tacky theme park

But then
At the back of the market
Where they were selling rabbits in cages
We came across a pub with an open fire
Full of drinkers destroyed by life
Broken teeth and mad hair
Shouting and laughing at the tops of
their voices
And when I ordered a drink
They turned round and stared at us
As though we were the freaks
US
Fucking hell, I said
THIS is the place

Dual Fuel Tariff

I received another cold call today
Katie, she called herself and
She asked me how I was doing
So, I told her things were bad
Really bad
*Oh, sorry to hear that, she said
What's wrong?*
Up to my neck in debt, I wanted to say
Two days away from closure
I'm rock bottom, I wanted to say
Surrounded by wasted lives and
Stamped on dreams

But instead, I told her I was only joking
Said I was indeed the person
Responsible for the energy supplies
And I let her tell me about their Dual
Fuel Tariff
Her soft voice was the sweetest thing
I'd heard in weeks
God love her, I thought
God help her succeed where we had
failed

Slam the Door

When I die, I said
I want you to dump my ashes
In that skip behind Lidl
Then go inside
Buy the cheapest wine and
Drink it in the street
While the good mothers take their kids
to school

OK, she said
We were at the table drinking beer and
I'd been drinking most of it

When I die, I said
I want you to break down in tears
Shout, there's nothing in the bank
He still owes on the car
And when you leave the morgue
Slam the door behind you
Slam it hard and blame the wind

She checked her phone and said she would

When I die, I said
Spray my ashes around the office
Let the bastards see what they did to me
Let them breathe me in
Then slam the door

OK, she said, like it was a done deal

When I die, I said
Pour my ashes down the pan in The Goose
Piss all over them
Then slam the door when you come out
Slam it so hard that people turn round and wonder what the hell is wrong with you

Will do, she said, and looked out at the street

A dog was barking
The traffic was jamming up
Life carried on

One for the Kids

You asked me to do it
Do it for the kids, you said
With your hot-rock eyes
Melting holes into my unholy face
So I agreed
God knows why, but I agreed

Dressed as Father Christmas in a cupboard
The hat too tight. The pants falling off
I put on the Elton glasses
And head out into the disco
To dance with the kids

They ask me if I'm really him

Am I a fake?
What do you want for Christmas? I shout
Phones, computer games, the usual stuff
So I tell them to be good
Tell them I'm watching them
And we dance to Gangnam Style

Then I feel a punch in the back
A tug on my hat
But when I turn round they all look so innocent
So sweet
Except the one with the cap
What do you want for Christmas? I shout
A machine gun, he says
So I can kill everyone
You're getting a doll, tough guy
With a pink dress
And shove him into the dance

These kids, I sing to the Lennon track
Need to learn some FUCKING
MANNERS

Half Past Ten on a Sunday Night

Half past ten on a Sunday night
He says, *don't read Bukowski*
He'll get under your skin
I won't, I say
I don't even know who Bukowski is
Until he pulls out a broken book

If you can't drink like a pro, he says
Sleep with crazy women, he says
Nail words to the page, he says
Don't read Bukowski
I won't, I say and check my phone

Half past ten on a Sunday night

The pub is a holding pen for the hopeless
And he's been my best friend for nearly an hour
He shows me a pad
Splattered with scribble
Offers to read me some words
But then loses his balance
And ends up on the floor

Outside, on the beer beaten streets
I check the kebab shop and see it empty
The owner slumped at the counter
Defeat written all over his shish-meat face
His empty-till eyes begging me
To come in and save him from everything
That's bad in the world
But we both know it's too late for that

Half past ten on a Sunday night
Nobody gets out alive

The Beauty of Litter

When you look at the pigeons
The crippled pigeons
And the litter
The wind blown litter
And the wing mirror
The whacked-off wing mirror
And you see beauty in it all
You know you're in trouble